LISTENING WITH MY HEARTH

A COMPLETE GUIDE TO ENCOURAGING CHILDREN EXPRESS THEIR EMOTIONS AND UNDERSTAND THEIR FEELINGS TO FEEL CALM AND FOCUSED ANYTIME

By Laurie Alber

CONTENTS

DESCRIPTION 4

INTRODUCTION 7

CHAPTER ONE "TEACHING GRATITUDE" 11

CHAPTER TWO "TEACHING MINDFULNESS" 24

CHAPTER THREE "EXPRESSING THEIR THOUGHTS" 31

CHAPTER FOUR "SELF-CONFIDENCE" 37

CONCLUSION 45

DESCRIPTION

T he book is a complete guide for teachers and parents to teach their children about the developing creativeness in the world. Children themselves can read the book to become encouraged about the mindfulness and cognitive abilities. They will realize the need for becoming more thoughtful and confident to stand in the competitive world. In today's world, the grades are not considered much compared to the creativeness and skillfulness. The book will touch every perspective of this category and will show the outcome for every perspective.

Apart from this, the book deals with the teaching of expressing yourself through words. If you can't stand or represent yourself, you have no chance of success in this world. The book gives a detailed tips and tricks of how to express yourself. It also mentions some examples, quoted from real life, to make you more interested in the topic. Examples can be a good source to encourage someone for a particular task or thing.

Furthermore, the book provides the significance of showing gratitude. It tells the reader about the ways of developing the nature of appreciation in oneself and the changes it can make in your life. Teaching kids the art of gratitude will make them prosper in their future life. In this category, the book quotes some examples from famous personalities to encourage the reader for practicing gratitude. Other than this, the book mentions some strategies to make yourself more appreciative. The strategies will include some random examples to provide better understanding and purpose of the strategy.

In the end, the book discusses about the necessity of confidence. It gives some tips and tricks to develop confidence for a better and successful life. The book also provides an authentic source to the reader, a study, about the confidence and its impact on life. It is indeed a fact that majority of the population lacks confidence. Just look around yourself, you will see many people losing their rights and conversation to other people. Many people are forced to remain quiet and are suppressed by the dominants. Many people don't take actions against the administration, they continue suffering from the strict policies and non-humanitarian working principals. What are they all lacking? They all are lacking confidence. They don't have the courage to stand for their rights and express themselves. Therefore, from the very beginning children should be taught of how to stand strong and face the situations of the world.

All the things mentioned in the book have some impact on your personality, so it is recommended to give a read with full concentration and will. For sure, after reading this book, you will feel the urge to bring the change in your personality. Let's jump into it and extract the knowledge for better and healthy future.

INTRODUCTION

There is a constant effort in making this world a better place for living. The people are thinking out of the box to produce things that are hard to imagine. In just twenty to thirty years, the world had gone through vast changes and these changes are unstoppable. Who are these people that are bringing changes in this world? They are no different than us; all of them are humans. They have the ability to use their creativeness to produce things that are not understandable by most of the people around us. They know the power of their brain and their skills, and they know the right way to implement it.

It is getting very necessary to teach our children for becoming more and more mindful, so they can also think out of the box in complicated or complex situations. Mostly, the children prefer staying in a cozy environment and doesn't want to explore their hidden abilities. They are either scared or not motived enough to step outside. There are many other factors that can be a hindrance in growing, e.g. confidence, self-efficacy, social pressure, etc.

In this growing world, everyone wants to be a part of the establishment and be an active member of the society. To be amongst the representative, people are standing and raising their voice. The representation scenario is everywhere; in your classroom, in your student council committee, in the parliaments, etc. If you are unable to represent yourself, you stand nowhere and everyone will consider you as weak and in minorities. If you want to grow and have a successful future, it is extremely important to learn the skill of representing yourself. Make sure that people don't take you for granted and should understand your importance. All this is possible if you keep a good track of your personality, confidence, and being more active in the world around you.

"It is only with gratitude that life becomes rich!" - Dietrich Bonhoeffer.

The above quotation has a very deep meaning. It tells the reader that be thankful for whatever you have and this appreciation will make you feel rich. The humans can't be satisfied with whatever they have. We will constantly work hard to achieve our dreams. Even after our dreams are achieved, we will start working on some other wish. This makes gives us more stress and tension. If we practice gratitude and make it part of our life, we will never have tensions and stress. All these diseases and aging would vanish away. We will be more relaxed than ever. All we have to do is to practice gratitude and bring it in our life. We should teach our children to practice gratitude from the very beginning, so they don't suffer later in life.

"Do the difficult things while they are easy and do the great things while they are small. A journey of a thousand miles must begin with a single step." -Lao Tzu.

Considering the quote of the philosopher, we will begin our journey to bring changes in ourselves and our children.

CHAPTER ONE "TEACHING GRATITUDE"

Before starting the chapter and get into its specifications, we need to know the meaning of the term, gratitude. What is Gratitude? Gratitude means to be thankful for whatever you have or be appreciative and return kindness. It's a quality that everyone should have in them. Gratitude is a feeling of being rich and better in every situation.

Mostly in class, children are trying their best to be better than the other student. They will try to copy them and will do anything to be above them. Here, the children are lacking gratitude as they are not happy for what they have. For example, a child in a class brings an IPhone and the other child brings a handset that it not up to that IPhone standard. Now, the child without an IPhone will feel lower than the child having an IPhone because he is not happy for what he has. He will constantly thing of himself as lower than him and this will make him unhappy and stressful.

If a child has gratitude, he will be grateful for whatever he has. He will never judge people and will ignore the materialistic society. A person can't be mature enough until he has gratitude in himself. There are numerous advantages a child can gain by practicing gratitude. Some of the advantages are listed below:

- **MORE FRIENDS AND FOLLOWINGS**: Having gratitude means that you are filled with a lot of positivity. You have no room for negativity and prefers to stay happy all the time. You appreciate everything, including your friends. You will give them respect and will thank them for whatever they do for you. Having gratitude means that you are loyal and don't betray people around you. In today's world, loyalty is rarely seen. This quality of yours will encourage other people to become friends with you. They will also try to follow your footsteps due to your quality of appreciation.

  For example, a stranger is holding a door for you and you thank him for his respectful behavior. This will create a sense of relationship between you both and a beginning of friendship. The stranger will have a positive image of yours and would love to interact with you (Positivity attract others!). Therefore, having gratitude and kindness will bring you more friends and followings. You will never get bored again with lots of friends.

- **BETTER PHYSICAL HEALTH**: This is the most important advantage for having gratitude in your personality. Nothing is more important than a better health. A study had shown that having gratitude reduces the aches and pains in the body.

How does body health relate with gratitude? Gratitude is a quality of being thankful for whatever you have. It means that we don't have to stress ourselves to work for extra hours for better grades or pay. If you don't take stress, you have a better health and calm mind. The chaos is the major reason for diseases and mind frustration.

For example: A person is working as a security guard in an organization. He stands and lifts heavy weight of the gun for eight hours to earn money for his living. If the guard has gratitude, he will be satisfied with his life and would try to adjust in his earning. However, on the other hand, the guard will continue working in shifts (extra hours) to earn more, for his satisfaction, if he has no gratitude or sense of appreciation (He will never get satisfied and will spend rest of his life working and working). Working extra hours without giving required break to your body and brain will cause pain and physical health misbalance. Always be thankful for what you have and ignore the greed for more. This will increase your life expectancy and your life will become healthier than ever. It is very necessary to teach your child gratitude, so they don't suffer from deteriorating health in their early age.

- **IMPROVES PSYCHOLOGICAL HEALTH:** Gratitude reduces a multitude of toxic emotions, ranging from envy and resentment to frustration and regret.

Robert A. Emmons, Ph.D., a leading gratitude researcher, has conducted multiple studies on the link between gratitude and well-being. His research confirms that gratitude effectively increases happiness and reduces depression.

When you are happy with your life, there is nothing that can ruin your mood or make you stressful. You will have a positive nature in the society and people will appreciate you and your presence. Hormones are severely affected by our mood, so having a positive routine and life will keep your hormones balanced. You won't have toxicity in your life and your life would be great. You will have a better relationship, a happy family, and a happy job. There won't be anything that can be the cause for frustration resentment or regret.

In case of children, their behavior would be perfect and they won't react to the situations around them. They will absorb everything calmly and will grow in a perfect way possible. They will have no disturbance and therefore, no depression. Many students are taking pressure for studies and grades. This can be reduced if children practice gratitude and appreciate themselves for the effort they put into exams.

- **REDUCES AGGRESSION:** Many parents complain about their children becoming more and more aggressive. There are many factors that contributes to their aggression. The biggest and most significant factor is lack of gratitude. If the children appreciate and accept their blessings, they will never show aggression and stress. Children should be taught that they should accept and stay happy with the things they have. This will make them understand their responsibilities and they will come out of their fake dreams. Try showing them the reality, so they should understand and interpret the true world. Practicing gratitude will surely reduce the anger and aggression in the children. They will become kindhearted and will have bigger heart for everyone. For example: A child believes that he should have a new phone just like his friend. He will talk to his parents, but they don't allow him to have one at the moment. The child will continue persuading his parents for getting him a new phone until he becomes frustrated and starts showing aggression. To prevent this, the child should learn gratitude. He should understand that parents don't think bad for their children and at the moment, they are not able to give him a phone. The child should learn to stay happy with current phone.

The gratitude will make the child's heart as open as an ocean. He will understand and accept other people and their perspective. He will appreciate people with their nature and behavior instead of materialistic things. The child will show no aggression and will be stress free. There will be no depression nor anxiety in the child.

- **BETTER SLEEP AND INCREASED MENTAL STRENGTH**: Of course when you are happy with whatever you have, there will be no room for stress, over-thinking, anxiety, money pressure, etc. This will allow the person to have restful nights and sweet dreams. Gratitude has a direct effect on your cognitive abilities.

"There is a calmness to a life lived in gratitude, a quite joy."

The above quote expresses the importance of gratitude on life. Let there be peace with gratitude. Sleeping more than eight hours a day is a surety to better health and healthy heart. It is said that most of the diseases starts with stress and anxiety. It is recommended to practice gratitude as it will keep you safe from majority of the diseases. Your mind will relax and will be pressure free. You can use your brain to produce other creative products or contents. This can increase your productivity and thus a better future.

Looking at the advantages we can conclude that practicing gratitude had great effect in our life, especially on our health. Gratitude is a quality that can change the fate of a person in no time. Gratitude can make you feel amongst the highest when you are feeling low. To make your life more relaxing and peaceful, one must practice gratitude. The following points will discuss tips and tricks for teaching children the art of gratitude.

- **SAY GRACE BEFORE EVERY MEAL:** In today's world, poverty is at extreme. People are unemployed and are unable to earn enough money to manage their needs. At every corner of the street, there are beggars fighting their situations. Children are homeless and women are striving for shelters.

In such situation, having a peaceful meal, three

times a day, is a blessing. Children should be taught that they should say grace before every meal. This will bring gratitude in their nature and gratitude habituated through practice takes residence in the soul.

The children would also realize the value of food and will stop wasting it. Whenever we order something at the restaurants, a lot of food is wasted and goes to the garbage. It doesn't mean that we should stop going to the restaurants, rather we should give away that food to needy and homeless people. This will bring self-satisfaction and happiness to you and your children. In long run, these habits will shape the personality of your children.

- **EXPOSE THEM TO REALITY**: This is a really powerful technique to encourage your child for practicing gratitude. The media is nothing, but a disguise. The children should be taken outside in the real world to explore and interact. Show them the people that are not able to live lavishly or are homeless. Show them a storm-ravaged area or poverty-stricken area. Surely, showing is more powerful than telling.

The children will relate themselves to the situation they'll see. They will understand that world is not equal for everyone and that they should be grateful for whatever they have. They are living far better than most of the people!

Your child will ask you many questions and will learn from them, so it is better to be prepared when taking your child to a storm struck area or a community shelter. Interestingly, your child will encourage other children to visit those areas. This will increase awareness and gratitude in other children too and will have a long run benefit in the child's personality.

- **BE GRATEFUL PARENTS**: Your child is reflecting you! This is because they learn from you 24/7. The child won't be grateful if the parents or teachers are not grateful. Try bringing a positivity and sense of appreciation in the house or school for children to follow. Be grateful for your relationship, be grateful for your job and house, be grateful for food, be grateful for your lifestyle, be grateful for the things you have; these things will add up and form the nature and behavior of your child.

The children will implement the things in future that are done by their parents, so it is recommended to have a positivity around the child. Solve your matters alone or somewhere that doesn't affect your child's personality. The people will appreciate the child and indirectly, that appreciation is for the parents and the teachers for better grooming of the child. Let your child set examples for other children and to make you proud in the society or community.

Be Grateful Parents!

- **MAKE THEM EARN STUFF**: The simplest way to encourage your children for practicing gratitude is make them earn for their stuff. To be honest, this method will make them understand the value of money and effort. The children will appreciate their parent's effort and will thank them for whatever they have done for them. They will learn to invest the money properly and will not waste them. They will hold their unnecessary demands and will help their parents in every way possible. The children will understand the situation of other fellow students and will support them whenever they need some help. Most importantly, they will feel independent as they don't have to run behind anybody for their needs. They will feel mature and grown up. There are many ways for children to earn money:
    - Clearing snow from the neighbor's porch or backyard.
    - Taking neighbor's pet on walk
    - Babysitting
    - Food Stalls
    - Selling old items, etc.
- **MAKE SURE THEY SOMETIMES DON'T GET WHAT THEY WANT:** This may sound harsh, but this is also an important step in practicing gratitude. If you keep on giving away things to your children they desire, they might stop realizing the worth of it. They will never be able to learn gratitude.

For example: A child wants a Toy and the child's parents get him one. After two days, the child asks for another toy and the parents get him another one. Again, after two days, the child asks for another toy and the parents get him another toy again. What is happening here? The child is not realizing the worth of your money and toys.

Suppose that the next time child asks for the toy and the parents don't have the money to afford it. At this point, the child will start misbehaving and will become stubborn. He won't appreciate their parent's effort for previous toys, instead he will destroy them. The child won't be happy with the current toys and will continue asking for more. It would be difficult to get that nature out of the child, so it is recommended to not fulfil every desire of your child and start teaching them gratitude from the very beginning.

- **TEACH THEM TO SERVE OTHERS & BE GENEROUS**: Teach your children to give away their items to poor, needy, and homeless. This will encourage to serve the humanity. Generosity doesn't mean to give away any item or belonging, it means giving on a sacrificial level. Give away something that they love the most. Real generosity is a huge step towards gratitude.
- **NEVER BAIL THEM OUT OF RESPONSIBILITIES**: Let them face the consequences of their action or decision, so they understand the difference between right and wrong. In this way, they will learn the

reason for gratitude. Don't spoil them by giving away whatever they desire, instead share some responsibility to help them grow in the world. If we think that the lessons are too hard, they will never fully understand. This would have a long run effect on your child's nature, behavior, and personality.

"Gratitude creates the most wonderful feeling. It can resolve disputes. It can strengthen friendships. And, it makes us better men and women." -Gordon B. Hinckley.

CHAPTER TWO "TEACHING MINDFULNESS"

In the previous chapter, we have discussed about the ways for teaching children the quality of gratitude. In this chapter, we will learn about the methods, tips, and tricks for teaching our children the art of mindfulness. The chapter had immense importance in children's life.

What is mindfulness? It means to be aware of our feelings, thoughts, bodily sensation, and surrounding environments. In another foam, the state of knowing about something. In today's world, the mindfulness is rarely seen in people. Mindfulness reduces anxiety, depression, stress, eating disorders, and sleeping disorders. Mindfulness disentangles you from reacting to particular emotions and thoughts as you become a non-judgmental observer of yourself.

Mindfulness can be practiced in many different ways, e.g. meditations, physical practices, mindful eating, etc. It is necessary to teach your kids the skill of mindfulness. It will make them more relaxing, appreciative, and positive. The mindfulness is a quality that can help them succeed in the workplace as well as relationships.

There is an emerging body of research that indicates that mindfulness can help our children improve their abilities to pay attention, to calm down when they are upset, and to make better decisions. In short, it helps with emotional regulation and cognitive focus.

The following bullets will help you teach your children the art of mindfulness.

- **ESTABLISH YOUR OWN PRATICE:** This is something that is necessary before you begin teaching your child about the art of mindfulness. You need to practice is yourself before teaching your child about mindfulness. In this way, you will be able to understand the right way to start the teaching process and the difficult steps in between. You will already have the idea of how to cope with the difficult steps and how to remain consistent throughout the practice duration. This will help you and your child in having a successful practice.
- **KEEP IT SIMPLE:** Don't stress it out on your children. Try keeping it low and easy for them to digest it. Make sure that the children like the

practice idea. Introduce them new games that links with the mindful practice.

For example: you can ask your children to stay focused and listen to the sound played by you. The sound could be of a bell, a set of chimes, or a phone app that produces sound. They have to listen to the sound until it is over. This has a calm effect on the children and a fun way to teach them to pay attention to their surroundings.

- **CREATE A MINDFUL BEDTIME RITUAL:** Practicing mindfulness at night has the most effect on your child's nature and behavior. Night time has the maximum effect. There are many ways to help your child in learning the art of mindfulness. The following points give you the ways to help your child in practicing mindfulness at night or before bed:

    - **Short Body-Scan:** Tell your child to close their eyes and sense their body parts one by one. This will help them to get more focused, more relaxed, and more relieved. A calm way to return to the body at the end of the day.
    - **Short Stories:** Tuck your child inside the bed and tell them a story that links with mindfulness. Tell them to stay relaxed and imagine the story in their mind. This will help them to absorb most of the story and store it in the

brain. Short stories are a great way to deliver something to your child.
- **Thanks:** Try gratitude, it is the best way to practice mindfulness. Every night before bed, praise for whatever you have. Be thankful for the food, restful nights, home, family, toys, etc. Gratitude has many other great benefits and it helps to shape your personality and nature.

- **PRACTICE WITH BREATHING BUDDIES:** One of the ways for children to focus better and strengthen their attention skills, particularly for concentration in school, is practicing with breathing buddies. Look around yourself, there are many children living in concentrated places with little to no peace. Honks, noise, pollution, etc. are part of their frustrated lives. It is very difficult for children from such places to concentrate and focus in the class or tasks.

However, there is a way to tackle this problem. The method is called breathing buddies. Ask your child to bring his small favorite stuff toy. Find a place to lie down, then put the stuff toy on their tummy and watch the breath go up and down. As the child breath in, count till three and then release. Repeat this procedure for five minutes. This is the self-management training and a great way to practice focus and mindfulness.

- **MINDFUL EATING GAME:** This is also the best way to practice mindfulness. Ask your child to stand at the door of the kitchen and sense the aroma of the food. Let them focus on the aroma and judge the menu for dinner, breakfast, or lunch.

  Another way is to teach them to eat slowly. Give a break of twenty to thirty second between each bite to notice the taste and flavor of the food. If they are holding utensils, ask them to put it down until they finish chewing and swallowing. This is a great way to enhance the concentration and focus of the child.

  Eating slowly has many other health advantages, e.g. the child will have a better stomach heath, absorption of food will be greater as the food will be better chewed, no bloating or nauseating feeling.

- **MINDFUL WALKING:** Tell you child that they can practice mindfulness even when they are in motion. They can sense the ground under their feet and can feel the movement of the body. They can feel the breeze moving through the hair or the clothes moving against the skin. Try focusing on breath when walking. This will help them to walk more and built greater stamina. They can even run a larger distance if they practice mindfulness.

Let your child excel in the world by practicing the art of mindfulness. Stay concentrated on the current situation and forget the unnecessary thoughts from your mind. Mindfulness is a great way to bring peace and happiness in your life.

"Do not dwell in the past, do not dream of the future, concentrate the mind on the present moment."

CHAPTER THREE "EXPRESSING THEIR THOUGHTS"

In the previous chapter, we have discussed about the ways of teaching the children about mindfulness. In this chapter, we will teach the children about expressing their thoughts. Of course, it is very difficult to survive in a world where you can't express yourself. Expressing yourself mean that you are able to deliver your thoughts, emotions, feelings, and ideas to another person or a group of people.

If a child is unable to express himself in a class, he will feel discouraged, low, and stressed. Everyone will make fun of him and consider him as a coward. Nobody wants to go through that experience! To become popular and active in a class, a child must master the skill of expressing himself. He should know the way to keep control of his emotions, expressions, thoughts and use it at the right time to leave an impression on the fellow classmates or teachers.

Nowadays, children are not being themselves. They are under peer pressure and media messages that tells them to obey if they want to become more popular and famous. To be part of a society, group, or a community, children are sacrificing their personal interests and tastes. This is killing the creativity and mindfulness in the children.

Teaching and encouraging the children for expressing their thoughts has immense benefits. Some of them are mentioned below:

Be emphatic and supportive

Perform better in school

Feeling competent, confident, and self capable

Less behavioral problem

There are many ways that encourages the children to express their thoughts. The following list mentions some of the most significant factors:

- **TEACH KIDS TO EXPRESS THEMSELVES IN THE ART:** This is a fun activity for the children and a great way to hear to their thoughts. Just give your child a blank paper and some color pencils, and wait for the result. You can use different music, dance, theater, crafts, etc. to encourage your child to express himself. For sure, every kid is unique and had different qualities. Keep on motivating them by cheering them up for their small achievements and efforts.

- **ENCOURAGE KIDS TO HAVE THEIR OWN STYLE:** In today's world, children are running behind famous personalities and peers to follow their trend and style. They are not using their mind and cognitive skills to develop their own style and ways. The kids believe that their choices are not worth it and lacks the modern touch, due to which they run behind other people.

  To get over this situation, parents should give choices to their children and encourage them for whatever they choose. Expose them to a great selection and let them select their own personal style. This will help them think independently and fashion their own style.

- **LET KIDS EXPLORE THEIR INTERESTS:** Don't force your children to select any particular field or education which doesn't match their style or interest. This would be very discouraging and would end up creating stress and frustration for the child. A study had shown that kids following their own interests had a better outcome rate than other children. Many children had interest of collecting pebbles and many had interest in reading books. Let them explore their interests and allow them to grow happily. Following your desired field will have a successful, happy, and bright future.

- **CONFIDENCE:** (Discussed in the next chapter)

- **AVOID GIVING INSTRUCTIONS:** Assign them a task and let them do it their way. Don't give instructions! Many of the children becomes frustrated when they are given instructions for certain work assigned to them. The child believes that they are being treated as a child and not as a grown up. They don't get the medium to express themselves and explore their cognitive abilities. This all becomes a hindrance for your child's successful growth and exposure.

For example: Give you child a task and let them do it the way they want. This will help the child to interpret his feelings and desires. He will be able to express himself more to you. Moreover, the child will learn from the decisions he will make. This will allow the child to successfully differentiate between right and wrong. All of this would add up and encourages the child to express himself.

- **LISTEN TO YOUR CHILD'S FEELINGS:** Most of the time, parents are very busy to give time to their children. The children love to share their feelings with their parents. They will approach you several times a day to tell about the way they feel about certain thing or situation. However, if you won't listen to them, they will start hiding their feelings and this will affect the bonding between parents and the child.

Give them time! Sit with them and take interest in their life. Interestingly, listening to your children will help you get to know more about their thoughts and dreams. The child will consider you as a friend than as a parent. In this way, he will show no behavioral issue and will have better bonding with other relations in his life.

"Always be yourself, express yourself, have faith in yourself, do not go out and look for a successful personality and duplicate it." –Bruce Lee.

CHAPTER FOUR "SELF-CONFIDENCE"

In the previous chapters, we have discussed about the ways for expressing thoughts through words. Now, we will look into the matter of self-confidence. As we know, self-confidence is all about self-reliance. It is all about acknowledging the abilities and capabilities in ourselves. In this chapter, we will discuss the impact and importance of self-confidence in our daily life.

It is a fact that self-confidence is all around us. From work to home to relationships, self-confidence is everywhere. How does self-confidence affect our work? The workplace is a battleground where a person shows his capabilities and skills. If the person is unable to express and appreciate his skills, the person will lose the competition at the workplace.

Imagine, you are working at a position in a corporation. The boss of the firm is giving promotion to a person from each department. He sets a criterion over which the promotion will be judged. Now, in your department there are two people only. Both of you are equally intelligent and skillful. However, you lack self-confidence and the other person is brilliant in it. Your colleague will be able to express his expertise to its fullest. He will encourage and motivate himself for that promotion. On the other side, you will be scared as you don't have the ability of self-confidence. You are not sure of yourself and your skills. You will consider yourself less worthy for the promotion. Moreover, there is a great chance that your colleague will convince you that he deserves the promotion more than you.

Workplace is all about fighting for you rights. If you are unable to stand for yourself, you will lose your rank and will never be promoted.

"Successful people have fear, successful people have doubts, and successful people have worries. They just don't let these feelings stop them."—T. Harv Eker.

Self-confidence just don't imply on the professional life, but also in your private life. Are you the head of your family? Or are you the most senior person in your family? If yes, then you should have the material of self-confidence in your personality.

How does self-confidence affect our home? You are a role model in your house for your family members. If you think low of yourself and your conditions, this will have a worse effect on the people of your family. They will also think low of themselves. Let's take a brief example of this situation. Suppose, you are a businessman with high status and potential. All of a sudden, you lose majority of your assets. Now, if you lose hope and the courage in yourself, your family will also lose hope and courage. They will think lower of themselves. Depression will fall and soon worse thinks will start happening. However, if you stay strong and support your family in hard times, there is a chance that you will recover from the lose together. The family's bond will strengthen and there will be no worse-case scenario. Furthermore, the children in the family learns from their elders. If the elders are not self-confident, the children will also be less self-confident. They will not consider themselves as weak and less capable. Therefore, self-confident begins at home.

Self-confidence just don't imply on your private life, but also in your personal life; relationships. I know it sounds weird, but it is a fact. How does self-confidence affect our relationship? Self-confidence is all about believing in yourself. Now, if you don't believe in yourself or you don't think you are worthy enough for something, this creates a barrier in your relationship. Look at the bigger picture and try to understand the effect on relationship by self-confidence.

You will have a limited role in the society. The society will gossip and will think low of you. They will take you for granted and it makes it harder for you to stand up for yourself. When you work on feeling better about yourself and having more confidence, your relationships will branch out. You'll have more friends and work relationships, as well as romantic ones.

"You're willing to commit yourself to the person who expresses interest in you. You become much less discriminating about who you choose. You may even be willing to put up with behavior that doesn't satisfy you, because you feel lucky to have anyone at all, even though you are aware you are not happy," –Dr. Lachmann.

There is a greater chance that you have less energy to put in your relation. To build a successful and strong bond, you should boost up your energy and focus on building a healthy relationship. This will help bolster your self-confidence. If there is low self-confidence, drama becomes inevitable and misunderstanding arises in relationships. It is important in a relationship to express your feeling and ideas, otherwise the relationship turns into a misery and frustration. To maintain a healthy relationship, self-confidence is the key.

In this chapter, we will discuss the tips and tricks for building and enhancing self-confidence. We are already aware of its significance, and so it is essential for us to learn the process of building self-confidence. The following points mentions some great ways to build self-confidence:

- **IDENTIFY YOUR NEGATIVE THOUGHTS**: Your negative thought creates a hindrance in your path to success. As we have learned in the belief system, the negative thoughts are created by the conscious mind and it has a negative effect on the subconscious mind. These negative thoughts can be controlled by our own self. It just requires some motivation and uplifting. To boost and build your self-confidence, one must identify its negative thoughts and convert them into positive ones. Think more positive than negative, give positive thoughts more space in your brain than negative thoughts. The subconscious mind is like a warehouse and filling it up with positivity will boost your self-confidence. Avoid spending time around things that makes you feel bad or lower your self-confidence. Take out some time from your busy routine and mark the things that disturb your peaceful mind. Filter them out and you will observe the happiness in your life.
- **MAINTAIN A POSITIVE SUPPORT NETWORK**: If people keep on discouraging you, you will have low self-confident. Your social pressure and fear will increase and you will not be able to interact much with the outer world. Let's take an example, you are a child whose parents keeps on discouraging their

child by saying that the child is not capable and is weak. Even though if the child is all good and perfect, he will feel sad and will have a lower self-confidence. This is just a small example related to motivation. If someone motivates you, you perform better. However, if someone continuously disturb you and discourage you, the person will think negative of himself and will remain in depression. It is recommended to keep a positive support network. Stay in people that help you in your difficult time and stand beside you whenever you need any help. "A person is known by the company he keeps."

- **<u>IDENTIFY YOUR TALENTS AND MAKE A PRODUCTIVE LIFESTYLE:</u>** Keep yourself involved in your habits and interests. Give yourself permission in taking pride in them. Express yourself through different hidden talents of yours. You will feel unique and accomplished. There is a greater chance that you will find compatible friend in your field of interest. Believe in yourself and start taking pride in yourself. For example, if a person loves singing and music, he will keep himself involved in the activities in his free time. He will have no time to think the negativity around him. Interestingly, he can earn from his interests. This will make him more confident and will make him more relaxed in a hectic life. Moreover, accept the compliments gracefully. If you have a lower level of self-confident, you will find it hard to accept a compliment from somebody. You will think that the person is either lying or mistaken.

- **STOP COMPARING YOURSELF WITH OTHERS:** This is the biggest hindrance in the path to self-confidence. In this world, nobody is equal. Everyone has its own potential, stamina, thinking, capabilities, strategies, etc. Don't make your life as your best friend's life. Think different and make a life as you desire than the desire of the people around you. Try to stand aside from the crowd as it requires self-confidence to be different.

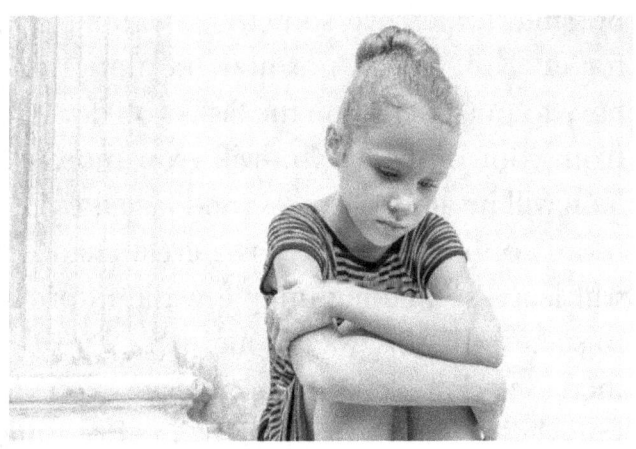

Let's take a brief example, if a child's parents are constantly comparing their child with some other child, there is a chance that the child will follow the other child than perusing his dreams. The child will go against his subconscious mind and will get weaker with time. His self-confidence will shatter with time. Always keep a card that is different from others, this will make you special in the society and will increase your self-confidence.

- **LEARN FROM YOUR MISTAKES**: This is the most important tip in boosting your self-confidence. Ego destroys the personality of the people. Don't let your inner ego destroy your impression in others eyes. If you work on your mistake, you will excel in your life. Don't lose hope by failing at one time. Keep on trying and trying until to succeed in your task. If you don't learn from your mistakes, how will you learn to improve? Think for a minute, is it possible to achieve something without even trying for it? No! This is not how the things work. You have to put an effort in the tasks you do. If you learn from your mistakes, you will grow more confident. You will be able to express and face the people with more confidence. There is a great chance that you will learn something unique while improving your mistakes. In this way, your extra knowledge will increase. People will appreciate you for your knowledge and wisdom. Learning from mistakes is the golden key in boosting the self-confidence.

"Each time we face our fear, we gain strength, courage, and confidence in the doing." –Theodore Roosevelt.

CONCLUSION

In the light of the above stated points, it can be concluded that children are a great asset that needs a great amount of attention for better growth of themselves and the nation. Nowadays, children are under constant stress and pressure of studies, friends, financial crisis, etc. They look around for mind peace and comfort, but fails which leaves a huge impact on their nature and behavior.

There are many factors that needs to be considered when teaching a child about the world and its cruelties. The significant factors are: Mindfulness, gratitude, confidence, and ability to express themselves. These factors are very much implemented in every phase of life and asks for great attention.

Gratitude is extremely necessary to have a happy life and soul. This makes you feel alive and burden free. Confidence helps you believe in yourself and your abilities. It allows you to excel in every matter of life; workplace, relationship, etc. Mindfulness allows the child to remain calm and relaxed. In this chaotic world, it is a great way to remove the negativity out of the mind. Expressing yourself allows you to represent yourself on many platforms and be amongst the highest of the society.

Gratitude, confidence, mindfulness, and the ability to express yourself are some qualities that can brighten the future of any person. Listen to your children and help them get along with their problems and complexities.

Keep on encouraging them and motivate them to perform better in life.

Let there be no stop for your child's growth and success. Move from authoritarian parenting methods to authoritative parenting practices. Teach your child to stop procrastinating and start focusing for better and healthy life.

"Children will listen to you after they feel listened to." -Jane Nelson.

© Copyright 2020 by Laurie Alber - All rights reserved.

No part of this publication may be reproduced or transmitted in any form or by any means, electronic or mechanical, including photocopying, recording, or any other information storage without the written permission of the publisher.

www.ingramcontent.com/pod-product-compliance
Lightning Source LLC
Chambersburg PA
CBHW070051120526
44589CB00034B/1974